# Pinchot Pass

by

## Bob Van Zant

With reflections on trauma, endurance, and the quiet heroes of the wilderness

August 7, 1974 – A fall, a friendship, a flight… and the long journey home

ISBN: __ 979-8-218-69900-0_____

# About the Author

Bob Van Zant is a survivor, storyteller, and seeker of meaning forged in the high wilderness. At 17, he endured a catastrophic injury while hiking Pinchot Pass on the John Muir Trail in the Sierra Nevada — an experience that became the foundation of his resilience, perspective, and voice.

Decades later, Bob shares his journey not as a tale of trauma but as a testament to the power of friendship, instinct, and the quiet strength we discover only in our darkest hours.

That strength has carried him through a second life-altering event, that of surviving the double diagnosis of bladder and prostate cancer.

These days, Bob continues to live fully – enjoying the outdoors, writing, coding, gardening, learning – and encouraging others to find meaning in the scars they carry.

# Acknowledgments

I would like to thank the following for their time, support, thoughts and feedback during the editing process:

Alice Crotty, Becki Craig Teramoto, Don Blasingame, Donna Salcido, Ed Borger, Gary Gutierrez, Heidi Van Zant, John Crotty, John Gilstrap, Keith Clayton, Robert Westberg and Sheri Lee.

# Table of Contents

# Prologue

There are places on this earth that mark you forever. For me, that place is Pinchot Pass.

It's not the tallest peak in the Sierra Nevada, nor the most treacherous trail. But for me, it's where everything changed—where a life on the edge of adulthood was almost lost if not for a friend who changed my fate.

On August 7, 1974, just days before my 18th birthday, I had a backpacking fall that should have ended my life.

What follows is a story written in snowy pain, silence, and courage. It's the story of a shattered leg, fading daylight, and a friendship so fierce that it held my life together when my own strength ran out.

This also is a story about what happens next— of being carried, being chosen, being saved, and being rebuilt. And it's about how some people, quietly, without fanfare, become heroes.

If you've ever asked yourself how much one moment can change a life… this is my answer.

Welcome to *Pinchot Pass*.

—Bob Van Zant

# Letter to Sean

Dear Sean,

I've told my survival story many times, and at its core is you.

You were there when I fell, holding my shattered body, giving me warmth and hope. You were just a teen yourself, yet wise beyond your years. You gave me a second chance in life; without your courage and selflessness I wouldn't be here to tell this story.

You held my leg together when it should've come apart. You stayed behind when no one else could. You never asked to be called a hero. But you are.

This letter to you has been written in my mind a million times, but only now could I put my gratitude into words. These words come after falling into despair over my cancer diagnoses and then finding my way back just like you and I did on Pinchot Pass.

Thank you, friend, for everything.

With deepest love,

Bob

# Chapter 1: Best Friends

We were high and deep in the Sierras, some 130 miles into the backpacking adventure of our young lives on the John Muir Trail.

We were 17. We were invincible. We were prepared for anything, or so we thought.

Our friendship and deep bonds of trust began in the sixth grade when we were the two new kids in our Northern California parochial school.

While Sean was an only child from a family of means, and I was one of seven children from a family struggling to make ends meet, we shared the legacy of fathers who were alcoholics and absent from our lives.

Sean was a gifted athlete with a genius IQ. He was quiet, often read alone at his desk, and excelled at all sports but was especially gifted at tennis and golf.

I was less sure of myself, shyer, and more gangly – growing ten inches my sophomore year and finally reaching 6-foot-5 by the time we took our trip. Like Sean, I also love math, science, sports and chess.

So, as our renegade spirits joined forces at the ages of 10 and 11, it wasn't long before we were hiking the hillside trails of Mount Tamalpais, building tree forts, and going on family camping trips together.

Although we each moved and went to different high schools, we remained best friends and in our senior year in high school Sean came up with the idea to hike some of the most inaccessible and scenic parts of the 211-mile John Muir Trail that reaches from Yosemite Valley to Mount Whitney.

We were especially drawn to Pinchot Pass, a remote peak of 12,090 feet that is one of six passes above 11,000 feet on the John Muir Trail along with Donohue Pass, Muir Pass, Mather Pass, Glen Pass and Forester Pass.

Pinchot Pass, named for the first chief of the United States Forest Service, also crosses the Pacific Crest Trail. It is known for its spectacular views, late snowpack and almost mystical pull into its deep crevices.

We had gone with others on a couple of short trips before and we were used to packing together, but this time it would be just Sean and me for six weeks.

Our planning began with us getting some 40 maps of the Muir Trail from the U.S. Geological Survey offices in San Francisco. We laid them all out across the floor at my house, taking up the size of the room at 8x12 feet.

We marked our possible route, scouring the topography for where we could bushwhack our way off-trail for more adventure. After breaking the trip into one-day stints, we made our list of food supplies, took on odd jobs to earn the money we needed, and even made our own granola for the planned 42-day trek.

Many of our supplies came from an Army surplus store where we got ponchos and first-aid items including blister tape and a couple of Carlisle bandages. Not sure what we were thinking that we'd need a field dressing with an absorbent pad and binding typically carried by soldiers to treat gunshot wounds, but we had a couple with us.

Our training included lots of personal workouts but also many hours spent running on mountain trails with rocks in our packs, sometimes covering seven miles or more through forests of redwoods and ferns.

We were ready, we had set a date, and it was time to prepare our food cache and take it to store on the trail. We drove over the Sierras to the city of Bishop. We had 200 pounds of food and supplies we were going to hike onto the Muir Trail and pick it up in three weeks' time.

We drove and parked Sean's 1955 Chevy pick-up truck at the trailhead outside of Bishop, California. We hiked one day to just below Bishop Pass above the timberline and amongst tons of small lakes. We slept there and then headed over the pass the next morning.

We really didn't know how this was going to work out or how we were going to stash our stuff, but when we got to Le Conte Canyon, we found a ranger that had a station there. He had a locker outside that was bearproof and could hold all our supplies – here, we stashed our supplies to pick up in a few weeks.

Three weeks later we came over to the Muir Pass and down into Le Conte Canyon where we were able to get our supplies.

Sean and I were pushing ourselves hard for this segment of the trip, and on the day before our planned hike over Pinchot Pass, we had done the punishing Mount Sill climb with its brutal gain of more than a mile of vertical elevation.

Our sights had been set on Mount Sill early in the planning stages of our trek. According to Starr's Guide, it offered one of the most spectacular views in the Sierra – a peak that stood not only in elevation but in reputation.

We planned to stage our ascent from a base camp between Mather Pass and Pinchot Pass, climbing via a route that would take us across a small glacier. When we came over Muir Pass and dropped into Le Conte Canyon, we spoke often about Mount Sill, both of us eager for the challenge and the experience it promised.

After picking up our food cache – Sean had made the resupply run into Bishop – and after my own first ascent in the North Palisades, Sean and I continued.

We climbed out of Le Conte Canyon, up and over the high, windswept Mather Pass, then dropped into a broad alpine meadow where we set up our camp for the night.

We prepared our gear and readied ourselves for the climb the next morning. There was no technical climbing equipment with us – no crampons, no ice axes – not even a rope. We had our boots, gaiters to keep the snow out of our ankles, and the shared belief that youth and determination would be enough.

Looking back, we were probably reckless, But, at the time, it felt like we were just keeping it simple.

We rose early and started the 5,000-foot ascent. Snow blanketed much of the route, and the glacier crossing – quiet, cold, and vast – was surreal. As we gained elevation, we eventually reached a landing just below the summit, maybe 500 feet from the top.

From there, the route turned steeper and more exposed. We scrambled up what was likely low Class 5 terrain – unprotected and fully committed. It was tricky, and with hindsight, seemed dangerous. But we climbed on.

When we reached the summit, there was barely enough space for the two of us to stand. The views were astonishing, but we didn't linger long.

Weather had rolled in quickly. Static filled the air – I'll never forget the feeling of our hair standing straight up from the electrical charge. It was absurd and hilarious and a little terrifying all at once.

After taking in the view and giving ourselves a few moments of quiet satisfaction, we turned to the descent. It was around noon, and we knew daylight was limited. The way down was slow and exhausting, but we made it back to base camp before dark – physically spent but absolutely thrilled by what we had done.

Climbing Mount Sill wasn't just a highlight of that summer. It was one of the most daring, bold, and foolish things I'd ever done. And I wouldn't trade anything for it.

After the punishing ascent of Mount Sill, we awoke fatigued on the morning of our Pinchot Pass trek but also reassured that the worst was behind us.

On our backs was our final resupply of 100 pounds of food and gear to carry us to the end. We were sore, and sunburned, and elated that we had stood atop the world together – just like we did in sixth grade when it was us against everything else.

Our young lives before we met were both filled with one disappointment after another. Our alcoholic fathers created embarrassment, disappointment, and sometimes just deep sadness. As I have aged and been through therapy it is always referred to as learning to survive and developing social survivorship experiences and wisdom.

Did this background prepare me for the unexpected and train me to survive under the most extreme of circumstances? I think it has.

Sean and I had triumphed over unstable and brutal weather that hadn't broken in weeks, leaving snow piled three to five feet deep even in August. We trudged on, our young and sturdy legs taking us deeper into the High Sierra and across Pinchot Pass.

# Chapter 2: The Fall

Sean was just 75 feet ahead of me that morning, chatting with a random trail buddy we had met on our 10-mile march to the crest of Pinchot Pass.

I don't remember the exact moment our trail buddy Jim joined us but from early on, it was clear he belonged. He had an easy way about him, intelligent and reserved, deeply capable. Once he paired up with Sean, they hit it off quickly, sharing stories and quiet banter as we moved through the High Sierra.

I could hear them up ahead, their voices drifting back to me in the alpine breeze as we climbed over Pinchot Pass. Although I couldn't make out their words, I could hear their camaraderie – two hikers sharing not only the beauty of the trail but the same mission: get home.

Sean and I had already discussed shortening the trip. After all we'd been through – the summits, the storms, the effort – it felt like it was time to pick up the pace.

We made the decision together below Mather Pass, in the meadow where we had prepared for the ascent of Mount Sill. We'd take shortcuts where we could, some risk, but we'd save time.

Jim was already in tune with us. Our steps quickened. The energy shifted. The long, meandering adventure had become a focused march toward the end.

Sean and Jim were in sync as they found an icy shortcut that would carry us along a steep ridge between switchbacks. We'd save time but we'd also be leaving the packed snow on the main route.

As they hiked within sight of me, I stepped onto the glacial expanse and immediately went into a slide. My left leg collapsed and bent my knee backward into the snow and my right leg flipped up and forward. I slid 50 feet downhill as my left knee buckled behind me and my right leg skated on the surface, my pack dragging behind me.

Time stopped, then exploded, as my body slammed into a granite outcropping hidden beneath the snow. My screams still echo in my head. But it was more than an echo – it was a giant wave of stabbing pain and white-hot anguish with a violent force all its own.

The cries that left my body filled the skies and overtook Sean and Jim as they moved across the snowfield, stopping them cold as they turned to see what had happened. It was a gruesome sight of blood, snow and a patella split in two. One half was driven into my upper thigh, the other rested beneath my shin. My tibia plateau was fractured, the knee joint was dislocated, and my leg was torn around nearly 180 degrees.

I knew instantly: I was not walking out of this.

Sean and Jim moved toward me as my cries of agony rang out. They each became silent heroes, with Sean quietly and instantly tending to my crumpled body while Jim, eyes wide in disbelief, turned and ran like the wind for help.

Without panic or hesitation, Sean went to work. He unbuckled my pack and rolled it clear. I was still embedded in the snow – my leg twisted behind me and my body contorted like a dropped puppet.

First, we had to move my leg into a position that wouldn't cause more damage. Somehow, we brought my grotesquely bent leg forward as I screamed again and again. The joint was dislocated, the knee destroyed, but worse still was that the bones had come loose. I couldn't see my kneecap. It was gone. What was ironic is that the whole time laying down after my accident, I never realized my kneecap was missing.

Then, Sean did something unthinkable. He looked at my knee, placed both hands around the joint, and manually reduced the dislocation – pushing the leg back into place. There was no morphine. No lidocaine. Just snow, blood, and Sean. We did have some codeine in the first aid kit, and I did take some, but it didn't do anything under the circumstances.

It was the purest kind of field medicine – instinct, necessity, and love.

We were still in the snow, 26 days into the wilderness, with no shelter, no Medevac, and no certainty that anyone would come. So, we came up with a plan.

I couldn't walk, nor could I crawl – not with my leg in that condition. But I could drag myself forward when Sean placed his hands firmly inside my knee, pressing the bones into position. And while he did that, I used my hands and arms behind my back to scoot forward, inch by inch, across the snow.

It took over an hour just to move 10 yards. It was 30 feet of screaming, blood and slush, and of burning muscle. Ten yards to a small granite landing, clear of snow, and solid beneath us. A lifeboat in a sea of white.

While Sean saved my life with medical aid, I later learned that Jim was saving my life in his own way. This stranger became essential to my survival when I took that fall beyond Pinchot Pass, high on a snow-covered switchback.

Jim did not hesitate when he saw my plight. He turned around, head low and focused, and set out immediately for help. No radio. No phone. No GPS. Just strength, judgment, and resolve. That single act – his decision to push forward and not look back – set in motion the rescue that would save my life.

# Chapter 3: The Wait

The granite platform where we stopped was no more than a stone's throw away from where I had fallen—but it might as well have been a continent.

It was solid, dry, and crucial. Sean had gotten me there with nothing more than his bare hands and willpower. And I had made the crawl through snow and pain—dragging myself across the surface of the mountain with a destroyed leg and fading consciousness. That slab of granite became our operating room, our refuge, and our waiting room for whatever came next.

The first thing Sean did after wrapping my knee was check for bleeding. Despite the catastrophic injury, I was lucky—no major artery had been severed. The damage was structural, not fatal… at least not yet.

But there was blood. A lot of it. And the wound, though bandaged, was far from stable. We had a well-stocked first-aid kit, and that was no accident. We had prepared for sprains, maybe fractures—not for shattered joints and emergency field trauma. But at that moment, everything we had brought mattered.

The Carlisle bandage made all the difference. Thick, wide, padded—it hugged the joint and held it, even as swelling and shock set in.

Then, Sean built the shelter. It was primitive—two ponchos, stretched and anchored into the rock with cord and stakes, forming a sort of open-fronted lean-to.

But in the High Sierra, where the sun can vanish behind clouds in moments and the wind can slice through layers like knives, it gave us *just enough* protection to wait.

I lay flat, encased in pain and silence. And Sean—calm, precise, quietly heroic—began preparing food. Even now, I can remember the smell of it. Hot Jello. He boiled water, mixed in the powder, and handed it to me with care. It was sweet, warm, and oddly comforting, a trail ritual we had carried for weeks. But now, it tasted like *life*. It did more than warm my gut—it tethered me to the idea of survival.

We had already been in the wilderness for 26 days. We were no strangers to discomfort, exhaustion, or cold. But this was different. This was triage in the middle of nowhere. And as I sipped that hot Jello through chattering teeth, something shifted. My body was numb now, but it was still *mine*.

I had stopped screaming. I wasn't unconscious. I wasn't bleeding out. I was there—and so was Sean. We weren't out. But we weren't done. We didn't speak much. There wasn't much to say.

Everything that needed to be known was understood between us—in the silence, the movements, the watchfulness. Sean never left my side. Not even for a moment.

At some point, I realized my body had stopped hurting. Not just dulled pain—*stopped*. It wasn't healing. It was detaching. I felt like I was floating just above myself, observing. I was still breathing, but the part of me that screamed, that felt, that *knew* what had happened, had gone quiet. Maybe to survive.

We didn't know how long we'd be there. A day. Two. More. We knew only that the sun would set, and the cold would come, and we'd have to wait through it together, and wait we did.

Time bent strangely on that granite slab. The sun hadn't moved much, but hours had passed. My internal clock had been blown apart by pain, adrenaline, and shock.

I couldn't tell whether minutes passed or lifetimes. I only knew I was still alive—and still lying broken on a mountain. The pain was gone, but not because I was healing. It was gone because my body had shut the door on it. Everything had become distant, slow, like I was watching my own story from just outside of it.

Sean stayed close, checking the bandage, adjusting the poncho shelter, preparing small bits of food I could barely eat. He was moving like a medic and a brother, calm and efficient, but I knew he was just a 17 year-old kid like me. He wasn't trained for this. He was just doing it—because someone had to.

And still… the hours passed. And help didn't come.

Then, out of nowhere, we saw movement on the trail, a scout troop of seven. Their leader, we would later find out, was a doctor.

They came up the trail and stopped at the sight of me—wrapped in ponchos, my knee bound, and leg distorted. Beneath me, the rock and snow were covered in blood. Sean talked with the scout leader as he checked on my wound.

Sean had informed them Jim had already gone for help, and it was agreed that the troop should move on as nothing more could be done for me.

And so, we were alone again. Sean didn't speak much at all. He just kept working—anchoring the shelter more securely, melting snow for water, keeping my spirits up however he could.

He made more hot drinks. I don't remember eating. I only remember the smell of the Sierra air and the sound of wind. I also remember one thing with brutal clarity. The body starts to feel like stone, not from death, but from stillness.

Lying on granite for hours—unable to move, unable to shift, unable to ease pressure points—your bones begin to protest, your muscles shrink inward, and even the numbness becomes heavy. There was no position that felt safe. There was only endurance.

I remember telling myself to hold on. Not for an hour. Not for the night. Just for the next breath, then the next, and the next. Sean stayed beside me, moving only when necessary, never far, never distracted. He was waiting, like me, but carrying twice the weight. He wasn't just surviving—he was keeping me alive.

Then, just as the sun began to lower behind the high ridges to the west, the sound came.

# Chapter 4: The Rescue

At first, it was the wind blowing or so we thought. Then, a strange, chopped rhythm, soft but growing. Sean stood, I tried to lift my head but couldn't. It was a helicopter.

At first, we couldn't see it. It rose up toward the pass reaching nearly its maximum altitude. It moved with purpose, but not speed. There was a controlled urgency in the sound.

It didn't land near us initially but disappeared around a bluff—just out of sight, the sound echoing through the canyon walls. Then, it appeared again, coming low: a small Bell chopper, compact and shaking in the mountain wind. Just a pilot onboard. No room for gear, no extra seats, no wasted space.

It set down about 25 yards below us, behind a rise in the terrain. The lone pilot climbed out and came up the slope to where I was lying. Sean stood and waved. The pilot looked at us both — me still laid out, wrapped in ponchos, leg mangled but stable—and nodded. No small talk. Just a quick assessment, and a plan.

There were two rescue calls that evening. Only one could be reached before dark. The decision had been made. The helicopter came for me.

The wind from the rotors pounded against the mountain like a heartbeat. When the pilot climbed up to where we were sheltered, there was no hesitation in his movements. He didn't ask questions. He read the situation like a field medic—quick eyes, efficient gestures, quiet authority. He took one look at my leg, at the Carlisle bandage Sean had wrapped so tightly around the shredded joint and gave a confirming nod to Sean.

Before they got me down to the helicopter, the pilot unrolled something from his pack—a clear, inflatable cast, like a plastic sleeve. He slipped it over my leg, sealed it, and pumped it until it hugged the shattered limb like a second skin. It held the bone fragments in place, stabilized the joint, and probably saved the leg from further damage during the flight.

Sean and the pilot worked quickly. Together, they lifted my body off the granite, me sitting on a tarp of some sort, careful to keep my leg straight. I didn't weigh much after 130 miles on the trail, but I was still 6 foot 5—longer than the stretcher, longer than the Bell helicopter that waited just down the slope.

I didn't see it land. I barely saw it at all, tucked behind the rise. It was small, barely big enough to carry two people— and they made room for me.

Then came the extraction.

Sean and the pilot carried me, foot by foot, down to the helicopter. There wasn't enough room in the cockpit for someone my size. The only way I fit was with my legs split around the yoke—propped at an angle, supported, but very tight.

They lifted me in … Sean stepped back.

He had prepared our packs, sorted the gear, made sure everything we couldn't carry was arranged and protected.

He did that while watching over me for seven hours, building shelter, melting snow, stabilizing my body, and never once stepping away.

Now, as I was loaded into the helicopter, he was my sentry. Tall. Calm. Alone.

The rotor wash rose, and the chopper lifted—just a few feet, then up and over the bluff. I could no longer see Sean. I never got to say goodbye. I don't know if I even tried. I was in a place beyond words—beyond ceremony.

But I knew this: He had saved my life.

The helicopter circled upward in spirals—descending by rising, if that makes sense. That's how it felt. Plateau by plateau, the Sierra peeled away beneath us. We flew for 45 minutes, leaving Pinchot Pass behind, crossing ridge lines and tree lines, and ghost trails.

Below me, the wilderness passed slowly. And so did a part of me.

The helicopter dropped out of the Sierra as the light faded from the sky. I watched as the granite gave way to rolling hills, then dry foothills, then flat earth, and orchards.

Civilization crept back into view. Roads, fences, rooftops. I was leaving one world behind and flying into another, yet neither one felt entirely real.

The flight was long enough for the adrenaline to start leaking out of my system, for the chill to settle into my bones. My body wasn't screaming anymore—it had passed into a kind of suspended stillness, preserved by shock, Jello, and Sean's hands.

When we landed at a ranger station with a heliport, I was met by a full medical team. Paramedics and rangers. An ambulance waited by the landing site, lights quiet, doors open. I should have felt relief. Instead, everything felt flat, like I was dreaming with my eyes open.

As they rolled me to the ambulance, I remember noticing the ridiculous. I was too tall, at 6 foot 5. I didn't fit in an ambulance designed for an average body. The doors closed on my legs—literally—as if the vehicle couldn't quite believe the scale of what it was being asked to carry.

It would've been funny, if it didn't hurt so much.

The helicopter pilot, still by my side, was still saving the lower half of my body with the inflatable cast. That cast held everything in place—not just the broken patella, but the shredded connective tissue, the fractured tibial plateau, the flesh that had been torn open halfway around my leg.

# Chapter 5: ICU and the Flatline

Now, the team at Exeter took over.

There wasn't much discussion. No time for interviews or bedside small talk. They moved fast and efficiently. I was taken into a hallway first, waiting on a gurney, conscious but adrift, while the attending surgeon was close by me.

That's when I learned a strange, sobering fact: I was 17. And that meant I couldn't legally consent to surgery.

Despite everything I'd survived, despite crawling across snow, watching a scout troop walk away, surviving a helicopter extraction, and being conscious enough to understand every moment... I was still a minor. A child in the eyes of the system.

The surgeon asked if my mother could be reached. I told them, weakly, yes. They rolled me and the gurney up to a pay phone—still inside the hallway—and helped me make the call.

It had been over a month since I last contacted home. My mother hadn't heard from me in four weeks. She knew I was out on the trail, knew I was supposed to be somewhere in the High Sierra—but she had no idea if I was safe, lost, or dead.

Now, the phone rang, and when she picked up, it was me. Her son. Calling from a hospital.

I don't remember what I said—probably very little. Just enough to identify myself. Then, I handed the phone to the surgeon. I could hear my mother's voice—distant, shocked, layered in tears—and then the surgeon's calm, measured responses. He got the consent.

He then turned to me and asked something that felt like a punch to the chest:

"Did you happen to see any bone fragments where you fell?"

I blinked, confused. "No," I said. "Why?"

He paused, then answered with clinical precision:

"Because large pieces are missing."

I was taken into surgery quickly after the call with my mother. There was no time to waste. My leg was shattered, my body on the edge, and the orthopedic specialist—flown in from Visalia while I was still airborne—was waiting to begin.

The anesthesiologist worked efficiently. I remember the mask. The countdown. The blur.

Then, nothing.

Just silence.

I don't remember what happened next, because I wasn't there for it.

But I've been told.

Shortly after they administered the anesthesia, succinylcholine, my heart stopped. Cardiac arrest.

One minute and twenty seconds—no pulse, no breath, no rhythm. I had survived a 50-foot fall, a shattered knee, a helicopter evacuation, and over seven hours exposed in the snow—and now, I flatlined on the operating table.

They worked on me fast. They brought me back. But it was close—too close.

In those 80 seconds, the doctors and nurses in that small hospital fought for my life. And when my heart finally stuttered and resumed, they didn't know how long I'd been without oxygen. They didn't know what would come back—or who.

But I came back from a cardiac arrest. We later learned was from a drug disease contraindication with my genetic muscle disease, myotonia congenita. This was a hidden drug interaction that was not discovered until after my heart attack.

I didn't wake up until the next day. I remember nothing from the surgery, or the arrest, or the hours after. What I do remember is waking up to cold hands on my body, massaging my arms, my chest, my legs—two nurses working rhythmically, their touch somewhere between medical and motherly.

My entire body was purple. Not bruised. Purple. Discolored from head to toe. The kind of full-body trauma that only happens when the blood stops moving for too long. My circulation had shut down. My skin was starved for oxygen. My limbs were cold, dull, heavy.

Those nurses were manually moving the blood through me, squeezing and rubbing, waking me up not just from anesthesia—but from death.

They spoke softly, as if I were a child. As if I might not be fully there. And maybe I wasn't. I don't know how much of me had made it back. But I was awake.

I looked down and saw the cast. My entire left leg—from groin to foot—was sealed in white plaster, heavy and unforgiving. Beneath it, I could feel the pressure, the ache, the strange sensation of a limb that no longer felt like it belonged to me.

I knew something terrible had happened. But no one told me everything. At least not yet.

Days passed in the ICU. I wasn't moved. I was monitored constantly. Tubes, wires, charts. I was awake, but not alert. I wasn't in pain—just detached, like I was living under a layer of fog. There was no moment of clarity, no grand realization. Just a slow climb back into my body.

It wasn't until later that I learned the full extent of what had been done. The two halves of my patella—my kneecap— had been in opposite ends of my leg: one lodged in the upper thigh, the other under my shin. The surgeon had retrieved both fragments, aligned them as best he could, and screwed them back together. He rebuilt my knee—and it's still mine to this day.

The pain would come. The recovery. The scars. But in that first awakening, all that mattered was that I was here. Still in the world. Still breathing. Still me.

I turned 18 in the ICU at Exeter Memorial Hospital, a full leg cast anchoring me to the bed, monitors ticking beside my head, the air around me sterile and still. There were no candles. No gifts. Just the sound of machines and the quiet shuffle of nurses' shoes on linoleum.

It was supposed to be the first day of adulthood. A milestone. Instead, it felt like the first day after everything else had been stripped away.

I don't remember much about that morning. The clock moved differently in the ICU. My body was too tired, my mind was too fogged by surgery, trauma, and whatever had kept me alive. But at some point, the door opened. And they came.

My mother and four of my siblings arrived with cake and cards and presents. My other brother and sister were working and unable to get away to see me, but I knew I would see them soon.

I hadn't spoken to any of them in over a month—26 days on the trail, and they'd heard nothing. For them, it was silence. For all they knew, I could have disappeared into the mountains forever. And now, here I was. Thin. Pale. Immobilized. Alive.

The room filled with the warmth and worry of a family that had been holding its breath for weeks. There were tears, but not dramatic ones—the quiet kind, the ones that slip out between sentences and fall into the corners of hospital sheets.

There were no "Happy Birthdays." Not in the traditional sense. But in every voice, every hand on mine, every wide-eyed sibling standing at the edge of the bed, I could hear something deeper.

You're still here.

# Chapter 6: Sean Comes Back, Life Goes On

And then, Sean arrived.

The last time I saw him, I was being lifted into a helicopter with my shattered leg dangling between the yoke, and he was standing alone in the snow, our packs at his feet, the Sierra at his back. He had stayed behind—no choice, no glory, no promise of thanks.

And now he was here.

He walked into the hospital room like someone who had carried a weight that no 17 year old should ever bear. He didn't need to say anything. He'd already said everything that mattered—with his hands, his time, his silence.

We looked at each other, and there was nothing awkward, nothing broken, just this understanding.

"We made it."

Sean had hiked out alone. Navigated the wilderness. Found his way back to civilization after saving my life. He didn't do it for recognition. He did it because that's who he was.

And now, here he stood on my birthday—not to celebrate, but to complete something we'd started together high above Pinchot Pass.

Later, I would learn more. I would learn how the helicopter team had to choose between two rescues, with only 90 minutes of light left in the day for a round-trip flight. And they chose me.

I would learn how my leg had to be rebuilt, not just repaired—how my own kneecap had been recovered from two separate places inside my leg and screwed back together.

And I would learn that even though I had turned 18 in a hospital bed, my life was only just beginning again. Not as a hiker. Not as a patient. But as a survivor.

The days after my 18th birthday blurred into one another. I remained in the ICU, my leg encased in a full cast from groin to foot, my body still weak from trauma, and my thoughts scattered like debris after a storm. Visitors came and went, but I wasn't fully there—not yet.

The room was filled with voices, gentle movements, the hiss of oxygen, and the quiet reassurance of medical routine. Nurses still massaged my limbs daily, working to keep my blood moving. The purple discoloration of my skin had started to fade, but the deeper bruises—inside me, inside my memory—had only begun to form.

Sean stayed close. Not constantly, but enough. He visited quietly, sitting beside me without needing to talk. His presence was steady, grounding. I often found myself staring at his face when the pain got bad—not for distraction, but for confirmation. He was real. This had happened. We survived.

Eventually, they moved me out of the ICU and into a recovery room. It wasn't freedom, but it felt like something closer to normal was creeping back in through the corners.

I was allowed to eat more. I was allowed to sit up. A physical therapist came to show me how to use crutches, though I wasn't going anywhere fast. My left leg was entirely immobilized, heavy as a stone, and the cast felt more like a tomb than a brace.

And still—I was lucky.

Lucky to have kept my leg. Lucky to have kept my mind. Lucky to have kept my life.

But trauma has its own echo. In quiet moments, I'd hear the wind off Pinchot Pass again. I'd feel the cold granite beneath my spine. I remember the way my body went quiet, the way I floated in the pain, the way a scout leader who was also a doctor had looked at me and walked away.

There were questions I didn't ask. And questions no one could answer.

Years later, I received a short letter—typed, formal, official. It informed me that Exeter Memorial Hospital would be closing within the year, 1998. The place that had pulled me back from the edge would soon be gone.

It felt strange, like a piece of my story was already fading. But maybe that's how survival works. Some places disappear, but the people inside them stay.

I never forgot the nurses who massaged life back into my limbs. Or the doctor who screwed my kneecap back together. Or the heroic paramedic pilot who landed a helicopter with little light left and carried me off the peak.

And I never forgot Sean. He never asked for recognition. Never made himself the hero of the story. But anyone who reads this and wonders why I'm still here—he's the answer.

I left the hospital with a cast, a scar, and a silence inside me I didn't know how to name.

They'd repaired my leg. Screwed my patella back together. Fused the damage with hardware and hope. But there's no medical term for what the mountain leaves behind when it gives you back to the world.

You survive. And then you live in the wake of that survival.

I went home. My body began the slow process of healing, inch by inch. The cast eventually came off. Physical therapy replaced rest. I learned to walk again, to trust my leg again—not because I believed it would hold, but because I had no choice.

But something had changed. There was a quiet distance in everything. In the way I looked at trails. In the way I moved through crowds. In the way people spoke to me. No one could quite meet me where I was. How could they?

They hadn't been there.

They hadn't felt their body break and still had to move it. They hadn't been chosen over another for the helicopter rescue. They hadn't died in surgery and come back purple and motionless while strangers massaged life into their limbs. But Sean had. He knew. And even after the pain faded and the scars turned white, he still understood. That made all the difference.

The mountain didn't just take part of my body. It gave me things, too. It gave me a story—but more than that, it gave me a foundation.

When I say I survived Pinchot Pass, I don't just mean the fall. I mean I survived the days after. The long months. The disorientation. The pain. The fear that any loud sound, any snow-packed slope, would return me to that moment.

The mountain taught me how to wait. How to endure. How to suffer well. And how to accept help—not because I was weak, but because I was worth saving.

There are things I carry that no X-ray can show. The rhythm of rotor blades. The smell of hot Jello on snow. The silence in Sean's eyes as he stepped away from the helicopter. The feeling of waking up from death and realizing I was still tethered to this world.

These aren't wounds. They're anchors. Reminders. Every time I limp, I remember. Every time I pass a ridge line, I see Pinchot. Every time I look at my knee, I see that scar, and I nod to the boy I was—and the man I became because of him.

The mountain didn't break me, it rebuilt me. And I've carried on with its lessons ever since.

# Chapter 7: Life Lessons

In time, I took up swimming.

I'm not fast—but that was never the point. As my leg weakened over the years, many sports I once loved became impossible. I had always wanted to swim, and with running and tennis off the table, it was time to reinvent myself.

I started late—at age 37—joining a Masters swim team at Joinville Pool in San Mateo, California, an odd 25-meter pool tucked into a working-class neighborhood. I joined the group jokingly referred to as the "90 and older" lane. Swimmers my age filled lanes 5 through 8. I was in lane 1.

The men and women I swam with weren't just older—they were experienced. Accomplished swimmers. Record-holders in their age groups. They became my mentors.

They taught me how to swim. They corrected my strokes, encouraged me when I struggled, and set an example of what was possible at any age. I was clumsy, slow, and stubborn—but I listened. And I kept showing up.

At first, I swam 100 meters in over three minutes. It was brutal. But I kept at it. Day after day. Eventually, stroke by stroke, I moved from lane 1 to lane 2, and so on. Years later, I swam a 1:14 100 meters at a long-course national championship in a 4x100 relay. It still wasn't fast—but it was hard-earned.

That one-minute swim was the product of 10 years of daily training. I learned to love water, love the rhythm of the stroke, and love the person I was becoming.

I started entering swim meets. Then, open-water swims. I swam a one-mile race and a two-mile race at Lake Berryessa, California. I swam Lake Del Valle. I did a Trans-Tahoe relay.

But I always needed the next challenge—something to test me. That's when Alcatraz entered my mind. It was 1999. I had been swimming since 1993. I remembered stories about my dad swimming at Seal Rock in San Francisco. No wetsuit—just another mammal in the sea. Now, it was my turn. I was the mammal.

At age 43, I signed up for the Alcatraz swim.

That day was a weather day. Fifteen-foot swells rolled through the bay. Seventeen-knot winds whipped whitecaps across the water. And the water temperature? A chilling 49 degrees.

It was just me, my Speedo, and my goggles. No wetsuit.

We jumped off the ferry—about 15 feet down just before I hit the surface of the water. I plunged deep, sinking 10 feet below the surface, and felt my heart and lungs tighten. Collapsing. Shocked by the cold. But then I did what I've always done. I reached down inside myself and surfaced. I came up in full stroke, breathing into the frigid chop, forward into the chaos.

It took four or five minutes, but eventually I numbed out. My body adjusted. I had prepared for this. I had trained in the San Francisco Bay waters of Burlingame. Swam in the surf of Half Moon Bay. Practiced at Aquatic Park in San Francisco—all in skins. No wetsuit. Just like my dad.

I was 6'5" and 235 pounds—carving through the cold. Forty-five minutes later, I climbed out of the water and sprinted through the finish line.

That swim was the culmination of years of transformation. From a broken-legged hiker to a determined swimmer. From fear to strength.

Why? Why go through all that?

Because I've always been athletic. Always outdoors. Always chasing the next mountain—literally or figuratively. I couldn't run anymore. Tennis wrecked my knee. But swimming? Swimming healed it. Strengthened it. Built up my calves and quads. My knee felt better in the pool than it ever did on land.

I was pressing myself hard. Swimming 3,500–4,000 meters, five days a week. Hard workouts. Tough sets. No pain. Just self-discipline and drive.

I eventually completed five Alcatraz swims over a 20-year period.

And when I trained for Alcatraz, I drew on the same well of experience that helped me survive Pinchot Pass. That same instinct to keep going. To adapt. To fight.

Swimming became more than a sport—it was a way to prove that I could still evolve. Still overcome. Still survive.

Later, when the cancer came, I had to let the water go for a while. My training became treatments. My discipline shifted from swimming sets to survival regimens. But the same fire that got me out of that alpine basin, the same discipline that pulled me across that icy stretch of water from Alcatraz—that was the same drive I would need to survive once more.

Just like the mountains, just like the trail, just like the San Francisco Bay — life keeps throwing cold water at you.

But I've learned something:

If you sink deep enough, if you reach down far enough, you'll always come back up—buoyed not just by water, but by the will to fight.

# Chapter 8: Reflections

Friendship and surviving were my saviors. That friendship taught me to value, treasure and preserve friendships forever. To this day I have many close friends, and I still have Sean, a dear friend that I talk to most days, here 50 years later.

After living with my repaired knee, I have had the joy and adventures of biking, swimming, playing tennis, running through forests and so much more. It has also come with its limitations, with pain, discomfort and now with the inability to do many of those things anymore.

My knee is not the only thing that I survived. In 2021, I was diagnosed with both bladder and prostate cancer. It's a bit ironic, but my treatments, which were extensive, were no different than the methodical process I followed from accident to full recovery of my knee. One small step or scrunch across the snow at a time.

I am cured and a survivor of cancer. It took multiple surgeries, one to remove the tumor in my bladder and another to remove my prostate. I also had 12 BCG injection treatments over a year, 38 radiation treatments, and 80 two-hour hyperbaric oxygen chamber treatments.

I am in the smallest percentage, 3%, of prostate radiation patients to get radiation cystitis, which is damage to the bladder walls, which I have today. I endured months of catheters, bags, and tubes off and on for seven months.

Whether lying on my back staring up at Pinchot Pass that I had just traversed or lying in a cancer treatment center, it is all about a mindset to survive, to overcome, and to conquer anything.

And to know that you wear some scars on the outside. Others, they live deep inside, tucked between memory and muscle.

I still have the same kneecap they found in pieces inside my leg and I am still walking on the same leg that shattered against granite. And I still think of that day—August 7, 1974—as the day I met both the edge of my life and the strength that carried me back.

Time has dulled the pain, but it hasn't erased the details. The slide. The snap. The scream. Sean's hands. The ponchos. The taste of hot Jello on snow. The sound of a helicopter when you thought no one was coming. A pay phone in a hospital hallway. And the quiet question from a surgeon: *Did you see any more fragments where you fell?*

I didn't.

But I've seen what stayed behind.

The love of a friend who never let go. The urgency of strangers who acted without fanfare. The invisible line between being a hiker and becoming a survivor.

And now, all these years later, I tell this story in full—not just for myself, but for everyone who has ever wondered if they'd make it through something impossible. You can. I did.

But you won't do it alone.

There will be someone—maybe a friend, maybe a stranger—who runs down the trail when you're broken. Someone who hangs in there all day, holding you together. Someone who picks up your call from a hospital hallway and says *yes*.

If you're lucky, you'll live to say thank you.

If you're blessed, you'll live to tell the story.

And if you're me, you'll never walk through the wilderness again without whispering:

"I remember. I'm still here."

www.ingramcontent.com/pod-product-compliance
Lightning Source LLC
Chambersburg PA
CBHW021148020426
42331CB00005B/954